LIGHT BEARING
Heather Woods

SPUYTEN DUYVIL

New York City

ISBN 978-1-941550-48-9

Cover photo: Rob Lendvai
Author photo: Tamara Trejo
Cover design: t thilleman

Library of Congress Cataloging-in-Publication Data

Woods, Heather, 1977-
  [Poems. Selections]
  Light bearing / Heather Woods.
    pages cm
  ISBN 978-1-941550-48-9
  I. Title.
  PS3623.O67625A6 2015
  811'.6--dc23
                              2015006951

Acknowledgements

Thanks be to these luminous beings:

Toni Mirosevich, for her insightful reading and vital guidance.

T Thilleman—generous spirit—who vaulted Light into bearing.

Truong Tran, who inspired the beginning.

Aaron Shurin. Elizabeth Robinson. D. A. Powell. Susan Gevirtz. Norma Cole. David Bromige.

James Kimbrell. Jack Finefrock. Gabby Glancy. Carol Clark. Maxine Chernoff. Jean Blacker.

Katherine Wallace. Katie Parry. Megan O'Patry. Carla Hall. Alissa Bell.

The Salinger-Nimni-Browns. Daryn O'Patry. Rob Lendvai. Anne & Jim Koch. Shotsy Faust.

Marcia Woods, for her steadfast faith. James Woods, stalwart. Mardi Gates.

Jan Gray & Barbara LaVey. Cully & Miro Desa. Kari DeLeeuw.

Chaundra Prehara. Carolyn Luu. j/j hastain. Rebecca Green.

Tamara Trejo & the Moon Mothers, for manifesting ether-real.

Heather & Hugo Pereira, for their prayers. Hanzel Pereira & Dan Hersey.

Reverends Jeff & Diana Cheifetz, for their spiritual guidance & friendship.

The members of the Swedenborgian Church, San Francisco,

who offered a resonant home in which to chase Light.

And to Geoff Desa, who bore with me through the Light,

from nascence to zenith.

memorare

fortula

"light of God"

lu•men | ˈloōmɘɘn |

    1. *noun.* (*pl.* **lumina** | -mɘɘnɘɘ|) Anatomy

        The *inner open space* or cavity of a tubular *organ,* as of an *intestine, blood vessel, artery, or vein.*

        ORIGIN late 19th cent.: Latin lūmen (stem lūmin-) light, window, literally *'opening.'*

.   .   .

A stranger realizes it's a perfect day and leaps to cover each lumen with her own body, while an entire galaxy of broken glass moves through her nerves. (Heaven is not what you think: no velvet zenith— more like the animal pain of mothers arriving at polished walls)—prayers—wasted—turn fingers into weeds in the downed day.

.   .   .

Marginalia: on reaching the distance she confessed. (Some say there is no tunnel of light.) (Some say we are merely vibrations.) History found a body to move the lever and pulped the words onto paper.

CONTENTS

Whatever the **lantern**

ripped open

and its wound.

flushed with vocal soothing

and with touch

tenderly, between the lines,

bled,   *the lines.*

There came a night

grave shook—and rocked

my spirit out—its glove

parted the naked skin

let terror in—until

a presence rapt—

my supple snapt body

so hole—so gaped

her secret place—

combusted face—

in mirror an Abyss

I let my seams tear

Out their hair

And in you came

And light shook too

dear world pardon me

make clear to You my

do not abandon

my hiding place bowed down

wait for the

even more fruitful

I will serve You if I can hear

the spirit and the bride say come

May I be free from suffering and the root of suffering may you be free from suffering and the root of suffering (and You) may the sutra spoken away spring up from a living door where you lose yourself and enter the dream of night *God is in the slightest shiver* may we find the starry navel and stare in see how the stream looks back up at us your hair wrapped in laurel oh lost sister are those daffodils cowering on the reed-bed *God is a question** answering You bend down and kiss my— to know— May You unfold worlds in me words look back in sand at their tracks pitiful oh have mercy on my self loathing which is also Your noose weighed double we all know the threshold of the dead hour I crave blue hour when birds chirp holes in twilight softening silence the moment heightens her breath I take your hand step out azure as Your light rings *for every minute You are the minute doubled*

Luminary

were you bearing

the light

between your

legs

holding the light

between your

eyes

bowed center

from which You

radiate lumen

undulate airily

sworn deep

unshorn self

not entire

fill you with grace

Beloved come calm

my hymn

pitted divine

reaching for the

pit scent

cell sent

heart bent

here Our

sweet meet

All the children come riding
giddy-up on lambs
to see darling God

She uneasily gets out of her dress and underthings and she is a girl again, four years old and staring at the Christ in her mother's room. She touched his pink mouth, the pink rent in his side, and then she touched her own mouth. She touched underneath her skirt.

I knew the saints

slip by my house I sip their aquatics bless me

Mother Thunder on the wall where I hang

His hands are etched with us his hands reveal

the naked Stream where what is washed says

Grace what is wished takes place the spirit

on your tongue may harm the body you turn

to me in a dark plunder whose breath your

turn raps my Lips never hear you rock

wrap around my rod alone and spare

the Rod coil the bile limping wing

Sparrow heat this wild loop child

Playing hide and seek with God

go around lick the curtains

trace His residue

you are hot upon the scent

I straddle the mountains

Goldilocks licks her breath

and who sits hunkered

corner seeker

I met a seer

who found You

or radiant remnants

blood nape

do you bleed

I would sniff each

luminous corpuscle

so close to Your—

Dear God I will serve you if I can hear

the spirit and the bride say Come

wander through Lips imparting snow

butter wouldn't melt in her hole

If I listen to them, You cramp my smile

If I listen to You, I do

and the science of aether so holy

your breath on my heart

Teach me to care and not to care

Teach me to sit still

even among these hawks

opossum play dumb

now's not the time to make fun

Hurry up please it's time!

daylight dawning dusk

your inmost musk I crave

God on your Word

the first bird alights

Playing hide and seek with God go around lick the curtains trace His residue you are hot upon the SCENT ever so lightly TIPTOE WITH GOD under her dress the white dogs CARESS YOUR HEAD I straddle the mountains goldilocks licks her breath BLOSSOM MOTHS appear through each other LIGHT passing through your head MISCARRIES bone for fur WHO sits hunkered corner seeker shadow streaker NOW COUNT to ten and I'll come out ready one two ten MIST was the MUSIC who shook God out of you

Those who don't believe

                                        call You my fairytale

But the voice I heard late nights

                        within her

flowery bed
                                                            so reel

            Sweet night cum shining

                                        ardor all for me

            Odor of clemency

                                                    I swoon over moon

You catch my palling star

                                        put me in your pocket

            Oh taste and
            See

my astral flowering

                                        release melodic steam

Every one hears You

                                             kiss me awake

The house in the woods

                                                  made of pearls

           blue milk morning   light
                         takes

Her first breath

                                                birds whisper

                                               Make any bed
                                      they're all warm

*I **want***
you to have
this,

all the beauty in my eyes, and the grace of my mouth,
all the splendor of my strength,

all the
wonder of the musk parts
of my
body,

for are we
not talking about real love, real
love?

In temple

they tell me

to not let herself get carried away

in a frenzy

but I cannot abide

such dull

love of you

I wish to be inhabited

Rub myself with your wild

essential oils

Now all my caverns

bask in you

manuka scent

just rained after

rough terrain

I am colored with your hue

sweet dusk echoes through

each of her padas

I am your gopi

your cowherd girl

My songs are drenched

with want of you

She streaks in streets

Unclothed ecstasy

and for this they

give me poison

which I heat into

luminous feathers

at night my bed

is laced with nails

which grow into rose petals

I can't mistake the guarding gift

of your scent on my sighs

Dear God I want
to nuzzle your—
So muzzle my—
Sap my stomach
Rip ooze and pour
from the interior
where the swarm
rounds me to ash
I have sown psalms
of the plea
Come in
I lift up my skirt
wish to know You
everywhere your
soar hesitant
wing of canticle
mounting my thirst
flame hush eyes
my tuft lit
summon sermon
swell in

What would you do with me

If I came 'in white'

Would you faint the Sky

clip Robin's song

I can hear you gasp

Watching my meek petals

tremble to light

It's a dawning I don't dare

except through this—

And in every timbreled Blue hour

I hear you humming just before

the song of morning Opens

Hands so cold no fire can wake them

but I can wait no more—wait

till my hazel hair is dappled—

So my dress remains dark

and the sky does not shiver

dear one—meet me behind—weeping echo—feel intently for the—listen—wind trembles trees into timbrels—soft beating—will I be yours—awe Yes—we will commit luminous chaos together and render havoc holy—all brine and sweaty shadow—quiver my bloodroot—You reap me—in conjugal visits—my habit off—creating a new ritual undress—Sweetness— of the bare moment—when you take me in Your—alms—that realm I go—clearing the reeds—inner ear beading for Your— whisper

This light bearing Your name
is made of me
flesh stamped Evensong
bulbous luminosity
dipped in Your velocity
I stroke Your vespers
get you off
The good book, into me

Hive of honey bee

expanded and I

dissolved in a vortex of sweetness

Fainting angel, I testify

The apple flower

fell far from

Her tongue

and out sprouts

His rod

golden glory

like a burnt out

honey comb

Her soul

So sweet the sky

Scrape through—

Pressing His light
into my psalms
fumble to mouth the
eglantine (sweet briar)
the way you droop after
vines tangle thought
hooked prickles
apple scent
Your bidden fruit
heats up my
heart a sauna
Hum-Sah
lifting eyes
(sweet musk)
masked
Hymn

I want to see you more—Sir—

There is little Luminosity here

We have a church in town

I never chanced to see

My cathedral is full

in her bosom

Yet how much fuller

I could be

If you came to me in white

Wonder wastes my pound

And I've waited so long

pounds are out of fashion

You said I had no size to spare

They want me to be thin

So thin— Morning—

stiffens her veins

The angel comes

to me knightly asks

'Who are you waiting for'

I say You— do You hear

I want to merry Hymn
The sweet burning

How His—
Penetrates all

The little rituals
we house

receive the body
that is Your word

alive from You
how crooked spark

over what realms
ignite treading

is how stumble
dusting the frock

out my attic
dawning the veil

each of her faces
You and your soul

contraction
wedding night

jitters shiver her
timber

meadowy laces
not a single one

easy to love
will you

God, are we there yet?

This road raw long.

I under hoof mostly.

Breastbone broke.

Head still.

Stow ache. Inner heart(h).

Missing clue.

God your androgyny

sticks to my pelt

I cream of you

walking about with

female bits

Soft like me you

nurture every suture

bloodlet and clothe the wet

with your warm reign

sweet blessed milk

And you too are holy

seen through

The wound in your side

gapes sew those who

peer in see

Your fecund

ventricle

I have supped on You

sweet with a tinge

of Salt

as if you had

been buried in

a mountain honeycombed

with naves

Sifting dirt salt sand

I dig you out of my

every cell

It is tough work

this unearthing

I sweat

and lose

dregs of You

Then lick myself

Take you back in

God, remember that time behind the—when You touched your mouth to my—whole awed and I—the shaking how it—Your musk pulsing the leaves—feel them quiver—my skin sees—light— a seventh sense—come to the edge—I—can't come without You— take these slim fingers— mossy words roll off—oh curl them round it—it'll be our little—gentle pressing—in two—head dapples—slit multitudes—loving You—in the afternoon—Your light through me—so moist— what was it You said—in my ear

You will know the happiness of being inhabited by your God

Enter her blood

Stream, softly He

(walks on water)

Whither it is going

Has to soften

(I believe)

and also you are

trustworthy

(who know)

her very sudden

motion (oval)

suture rapture

in the slightest

ravish (wound)

gapes Him

through

Light shattering
with her bare fists
Porcelain light cracked through
mellow edges
You fill me up such
that my seams would burst
Lumen distend
I come apart
in her seems
entrails shock
pull of light
And poems, hems of them
dragging along floorboards

I feel Him in my

bones

Light in it body

A surging sternum

We give off waves

red bells go off

The slightest sound

shiver her timber

When I say undulation

what do you hear

A wave unwaving

Such vibrancies

between Us

Sip sound of

Light one body

desire to conceive

vibrate revel

shaky rebel

one lit body

may cause

a stir

The soul is kissed by God in its innermost regions.

an instant

of doubled pleasure, **concentration, con-**

penetration.

Listening to God

remains the brute desire

Our remains scattered utterly

about His interior

drink it down velvet

uterine lining silver shining

I dance the flesh

arise in (arousing) You

I am your ecstasy now

Be a good blue and

      graciously enter me

My head which is a clouded clearing

where a little fecund what hides

      no Shepherdess guides

Around Her ankles, angled

thoughts tangle in kelp

Gather again in the house

      beneath the water

Sea weather is fair as my

      inner see whether

The breeze says I am the dew

The bird says I am the book I

      who am not says I see

The sucker says I am

      the humming

Part the peacock
breath between knowing
I rub peacock feather over her
and all my good besides
slipping realms of bliss
in spells a bell melts my ear
and leaked excessively
grasp and abandon
thunder oven flooding skies
plunder the light between
walls upon walls offer flowers
adapting to light gathering
the body to myriad peaks
A thousand eyes open at once

Tender thirst
breathes through
alit clit hum
alight clot hymn
He is here
Yes *there*

Kundalini

(cuntilingus)

release what was

from its coil

stored (shored) up

My 'subtle body'

condensed curls

chakra aspirant

climb spine

and kiss the—

held fast in

hole explode

the base of

your tongue

journeying upward

toward God

Wander through the
path You have cleared
For

For if the

streams full

know of God

her face shone light

chalked flicker

lambent hymn scent

hair pulled

four lips

small swells

undulate through dusk

Lick her quick

it up flame and oh

Light that is my beading body

hear my corpuscles pool

I am your ecstasy now

Your energy hush

creases in

flush You

quiver as Me now

never again

quite the same

deliver

God your fangs

in my neck

feel so good

Like they were always

meant in me

Without tongue

I move your head

And spitting rapids

gaze upon us

divine Dinner

My blood on you

The body works

Having no weight

Light shatters

blood stained glass

A silent flash

like death

I have torn pages off Your—

slit open my—

redeem this ecstasy

make all New

make all kNow

shout it off the rooftops—Lord

I am come

Your bride

***Much Madness** is **divinest Sense**—*

As I write this, the noises in my head are so loud that I am beginning to wonder what is going on in it. As I said at the outset, they have been making it almost impossible for me to obey those who commanded me to write. My head sounds as if it were full of brimming rivers, and then as if all the water in those rivers came suddenly rushing downward; and a host of little birds seem to be whistling, not in the ears, but in the upper part of the head, where the higher part of the soul is said to be . . . for the spirit seems to move upward with great velocity.

The Crazy douses my House in Twilight Calm of the Form with Water language out my Chest Heaves and I see God not heaven You Grown in her sleep stir syllables with water Cure My Body poaching the Born Corpse it is too much to be born Take this seed for spirit Taste His Seed and spear it all over your Hinge her cord smear the game Of love and how to Slay it forbear twinge your burned together Foramen chant but my eyes Impinge his Word at high tide Singe your lord Licks burnt wedding ring through which rose streaks Faintly Up sparkling little Wows there were Bells between the church and My Vow confident God will know how

Merry full on face,

The Chord is whimsy,

Blessed art now a ton hymen,

And blessed icy toot of my boom,

For sow hawthorn Shyster Savory-her,

The Tea-lover assholes.

Shamen.

Off mind Off I am what pronoun I Pronounce aspirated flower Bells there were Bells but I never heard inspiration Tower lick it The Suffering off mind off *Bhikkhu* like Sick *Dukkha* like spook After a Spell she came back to her cell again sum of my womb fruit of my tomb backing herself against His Shhh! I'm trying to hear you Imperceptible Orange Light Coming Out My

And the people in her head said

Amen

Oman

Āmán

: /ɔːˈmeɪn/

aw-MAYN

Ahmeen

Ah men

Amun

Aum

Amen-Ra

Raw

O Farter, hoof farts in oven,

Hollow bee thigh mane.

Thigh condom come

Thigh spill be dun

Unearth hasidic coven

Jib us today our pale lea bred.

Camphor river art reap asses,

As wheat fog hippos shoot rest past hugging tusk.

Manly does knot enter ten patients,

Butter liver us bus primeval.

For dying is ducking dumb,

In the bower, allegory,

For river endeavor.

Shamen.

Hell Merry,

Uberspace,

The Lard is witty;

Flaccid tart ow all hung yeomen,

And flaccid is tofu of thigh room, Cheese-wiz.

O lemury, Mantra seed Pod, stray from musk wieners,

Noun and titty bower dove our meth.

Shamen.

*What is to give light must endure **burning**.*

In the hither world I lead you willingly along the light-bearing paths. In the hither world I offer a once-and-for-all thing, opaque and revelatory, ceaselessly burning. Anyone who has ever been through a fire knows how devastating it can be . . . I was there. I know.

Himself himself diversify—spirit flapping in the—when I swallow round it—her heart scantily clad—her heat gone mad—pressed as if by some other—ether real—figment of my— pigment of your—God's whisker—brushing my—it's real I tell you—this burning in tempest light—douse—her hair— aflame—beloved—she is not in her— right bind—round her ringing—wrists

Quick

check her vital signs

panting tears

temperature

cold

deep breaths surfacing

He must be in the room

Measure it by her awes

every shaking limb

a new host

threw my legs Wide

mined joy

Is it true

her self heaps hide

gasping

her breath keeps time

crowning

Knows who

Godhead

Stirs in bed

His lips press

my

In her Innermost there were Others present and the body reaped light the room Flew viridian male breath chants Marry the Ecstasy now Take it between teeth or else know new realms of Your heaven is my hell finding God in my woman's shape curve of the deep Serpents in her gut oh Mercy please Handle me gently when you—it's you I curve into *The Spirit tells you what to do.* Light flickers my tongue I go to bed conscious of you I wake up with Your Breath in my body slither Guide It through Listen listen hard or you'll get bit

Tongue tied and speaking in

torn tongues forked fluted

the flavor of Hymn

I am like her in shadows

how all things

unless it comes

combing my tongue for your Word

renounce every disturbance

do Thou

and really I believe

red tongues moving in

my breastbone

Have you the little chest—to

put the alive—in?

I could build it for you

cedar scented and lined in feathers

Somehow the weight of the soul

And would you say 'crawl in

Daisy do'—would you ask me this

Bury her song alive

And the sound keeps coming

Out of the lock hole

Underlapping wrens wings wrestling for a vision tread a soft SOIL containing what spirit Her feet pumping the sound out pedals stop but the organ Keeps playing out of her— Look for the light you cannot see gamma ray gnostic fray light seeking star weeping the pigeon hears ten notes for every human one birds ear absolute timbre curdle my deceptive senses navel gazing star raising let me reveal You *Be shelled, eyes, with double dark And find the uncreated light* invisible wave length in-for red cluster all-true violets Moving at the speed of— shaking the sky out whoever enters me is not a ghost You earth rust You star dust what song is playing inside me star innards become you nebula near light year a shiver of something galaxics quiver You

Now I know the pleasure
of being inhabited by My lord
I will not return

Lock her up—
keep you taut
dandle you through
a gust of breath
neck hairs quiver
arias split ends

She is host
to holy Ghosts
and her breath reeks
of dew

Her agony

         Feels so good

to Him

Sweet ache

      in your side

Triptych

supple Stitch

Her mind was

    Like a dry board

  when it has been scorched

         Crying out

Lead us into his

   blessed breast

through his

      Sweet open side

[But Christ loved] her more than [all] the disciples, and used to kiss her [often] on her [mouth].

> (She of the see through spirit
> and peek and screw soul)
> I am the sweet holey virgin
> I am the humble whore
> You can't live without me any more
> I've walked with you
> feet weathered in sand
> hands withered in yours
> Their eyes upon us
> offer no solace
> You came to me for earthly love
> and found ethereal trove
> That wonder chest
> between her holes

Beloved I am parting

Tomorrow you'll meadow spread

only ashes to remember me

Mouth wide as the first urge

It's getting hot in here

My rafters burn and break

The lord our god is a

burning and consuming fire

Licking up my skirt

Soon you'll smell it

Even honeyed

hair burns

I gave— the blue
time— to shore
reverently if I
unmarked heart
hear Him through
a timbrel
blood leaving her
mind seek hymn
pour lantern in
but the tune
folded up—
chest alive
with the shaking

There's a certain Slant of light,
Winter Afternoons—
That oppresses, like the Heft
Of Cathedral Tunes—

I never meant to write of You

but You bound and gagged me to

this page: vast white desert

I fear I trespass upon your kindness

It's a form of brute force

putting words in her mouth

Watch it writhe in

Sweet disorder

Me, little mind

full of bird whistle

limbs creak against your

desire

a thousand lashes

for these words

I am a stupid creature

Cover her mouth

bird beaks peek

through lips

God You were my first

Remember it prescience

Your scent tied in my sheets

My neck crooked where Your arm

pinned me down rapt my mind away

Constellatory bruises

dot my arms

Lavender blue love trail

leading up

her (w)hole

canal gladdened

as You planted Your

revelations

sweet ache

star withIn

Where you had foraged

All day long

my legs are not my legs

the Flowers growing Out

reek of You

My mind has withered

from the root

And no birds sing

Enough for today
Lord I'm spent
wrists shaking
excessively small
droplets of blood
form a pattern
It's a cross stitch
fragile thread
a dying art
I don't dare disobey
You say
I've a Call

I spoke the light
to Him I breathed
Light in Hymn
I didn't hear you
listening and then
as if caught playing
one hundred pianos
I closed their lids

In the sixth canonical hour

she fainted

Her wrists without pulse

seemed to hum

Your favorite hymn

as a girl

Under the **light**, *yet under*

If I could keep spinning this way

(so quietly) and the birds would stop

their incandescent chirping long enough

to hear My thoughts and the garment I

am weaving would stretch across my heart

and rend the plum-song as it canter-

clops along Then I am sure the path of light

rays would extend past my skull and there

would be no My which surrounds itself with

Mine limited coo But all things radiate powers

radiant Now and the colors in a pigeon's neck

Are true colors

Please pray with me living one may the graveyard push pleasure up this easter feast your eyes on my—intense longing for the sound of the monk's bell drives out all otherly desires crouch down in the seventh circle auricular oracle you lure lyre pure gold strings lick lampwork little saints hypnotic dead turning my breastbone wailing women their voices loons lavender cracked what is the consequence of I moon reaper tearing the sacred up tuft by tuft eating her moon out I bend in the tall grass between notes

I am That Hum-Sah

becoming free from

whose mind is pure

eating the flinching

whole tit hold it

You have no idea

God is a presence

attainable by the

absolute Inkling

God is present

I saw the universe

divided in many ways

All present in my body

a fruit cut open

touch it *Hum-Sah*

seeds pink ooze

expanding the flesh

S/He abides me

Cosmos in chest

God in my head we are
talking something like
How does that strike you?
Right between the thighs
This little light of mine,
I'm gonna fret and pine
Arc of your face changing
after all these years
God, it's still You
who talks in my dreams
streams bless Thee
weeping over rocks
who made Me
skipping under hum
Your thundering door
leading me by the lyre
sweet graves sigh out
to be touched
what remains
the moment
pulled back

Who *seeks the flaw in everything and loves the flaw* my bride God is silent playing his grey guitar in the corner of mind meadow dear me gracelessly babbling my loves loathes *O to be self-balanced* if such a self I see *Grand is the seen, the light, to me* I am away from herself at present seeking unconditional love birthright light digging in sand vesper hand gesture aye for she's to inherit God's gaze there now Little One did you hear I love you replete and may return as a bird bone or leaf disintegrating the Spirit say come I scatter myself to find you honing over hill and dale our chorus chants Grant us the seed, the right to Thee

A speaking aether seeks

a blue pearl

seer between flame

spits in muscle scent

Dance and mend

trance and rend

home

After the ecstasy the laundry

after the sweetness the cavity

after the poison the peacock glows

my relationship with God is as complicated

as my relationship with self

O to be self-free

O to be self-balanced

No self I sing

and hang herself out to dry

silk on the line

such delicates are easily derailed

pin her up butter cup

self flapping in the breeze

tethered and tattered

light gets through

becoming prayer flag

Exit

at another point into the intense outer light.

Outside of my outside there is Another

moss rolls the stone of my thoughts not gentle mother

on the earliest tip of dream riding you gleam over

horizon strung with wave lit clouds

found space how to hover here forever

the rooster sings my awakening

gentle death knell now bow lit feather

like the one between my when you tickle low

or the sparrow this morning her wing breaks

I heal it in my

fog horns diminish her inner eruction

the pace of your feet matches my racing heart

when I see his Cold I heat hymn inner Hearth

I am a porn free zone

I can't live in anything moving too fast

I am a natural source of renewable energy

My core of luminous peat

I am a rainbow a covenant of Your love forever

bridging the gap between outer inner

Let this mind be in you

                                big sky mind

                I am suspended mid-moon

        kiss my full bloom

                voice of cloud and holy folk

call it spaciousness

                subconscious bliss

                        If unseen a cell

would the sky so immensely

                penetrate your hive

                                abundant homeward flutter

        I gleam to perceive

                lifting belly is so strange

    sweep and scour

            every living light

            will lay in your lap

                                up here my all overflows

                                    bearing divine bifold

        wispy color above now below

                            mark my Organs with chorus

                the sky perspires

        with a smudging and a blessing

Our liver aria atrial flutter

            catch Thy crescendo

                        it's a leap

                a light in the heap

        Oceanic teat

            tongue between teeth

A glottal stop

where you keep your hidden God

Light the flesh

eyes of flutter

Whenever you hear a blessing recited

chant my name

Tabernacle of bread and dew

You may not utter

We buried your sound

in the deep freeze

Our rituals keep your body

on ice

Verily I say unto you

be firm, faithful

to the Light you

cannot see

I am initial

I lack backward

reference

The scent before

Your eyes perceive

the dawn

The taste of words

embodied

in silent hue

Our lips blue

And so it is

God is unity

chorus of oneself

beneath feet worms

unearth aria

the seed of which

cells Gnosis rush

Pleasure fill daffodil

drips sickle drip

silver birds swarm

black branch quiver

How much thinking

can I bear without You

I confess this light

is breaking me

a bulb her heart

will make a living

Spirit who am God

the speed of which

inflowing birds

my mouth

Distilled longing

  in my

  (craw)

I am not lyric

(staccato)

aether hollow

ebb of Your

when you open my

unsung (song)

for (or) against

(pleasure) brush up

struck (pain)

Knowing these two paths

within you

unhaired silk psyche

mine unhurried

unharmed mind

God You

unarmed my will

thank You (I'm)

all ears (all years)

All Yours

May all beings be full of light and the roots of light (in fall such bright threads dangle down) may you be free from the hungry bird peering through the window (and I) may all aspire to know the scent between her chamber press balm to lips of (who is light) Hymn in all craw may a crow call remind you of being (now) may you be free from the duality of like and disdain (and me) of other spit against (Other) may our black eyes hit Him simmer (no sooner a sinner) may our eyes left out in the snow air be where peacock eats Our poison tail (behold) unfolds Hymn shimmer

I (*that cowde no letter*)

Am writing this to you

From a far away place

inside Herself

The room is cold

For we've no heat

I sleep on straw

My feet bare

The better to consume you with

inner writhings are hot

and send me in a spin

of such Rhapsody as I

never saw in child dreams

Your salvific grace

a ruddy place

where I am home to sit

You did not respond

but did you receive—

morse code with taps of Light

I spent my entire life

devising this—

A hieroglyph for just us two

invisible to all but You

Perhaps these words die

on my lips

Did she say too much

shy you away

I fear I cannot live

without your song

between these hips

(ink clots Pen's tip)

Come and take the fleshly vow

Stay inside me a Tinge

longer now

God you are homely

My foul and familiar

My *homlyhed*

You in the dank female corner

In herring scales

glittering on floor

In raindrops fainting from her

eaves

In the corpse calm contrite

I sense you even

In stinking mire

these hands are tasked to scrub

When I wash the dying

fish and

Cook her heart through

Night falls while the children dream

You are

When I saw that I and my body are not the same

I stretched and gave thanks evanescent home heavensent home You-rendered watch her moon blush vital signs virtual brine really so much dreaming in such a small house the rafters *unloose small bats and owls* swans wing bearing wall skipping hearth creep right her floorboards trip you that secret staircase the color of crumpled pearls glow up heals clicking vine tangled stair attic full of luminous suds flying buttress propensity of light through her window cast Your portents on my shadows nod-nod wink lusty sink soak it all in stroke her heaven-Scent kissing herself goodnight let's leave all the lights on flashing a mirror spirit so every creak is sacred every crease gate swings back as long as I live here

I am god-made
heart of the Ground
throbs
birds haunt my air
a woman fair and firm
dripping with firmament
bird tangled hair
prophetic locks
something loose in her
word bore Witness
He quivers slightly
stroking the Key
I am in you and
You are in me
shining the pieces
out, we star-Dust
we God-rust
See his Seed
in my tiniest—
stem cell
stellar bell
arch of sky
arc of breast
art of Seeing self
shining In—
Thyself a Sea

Notes

MARGINALIA

A stranger realizes it's a perfect day and leaps to cover each lumen with her own body ...

~ Marjorie Stein, *An Atlas of Lost Causes*. ©2011. Used with permission of Kelsey St. Press.

LANTERN

Whatever the lantern / ripped open / and its wound . . .

~ Barbara Guest

God is in the slightest shiver / God is a question/ for every minute You are the minute doubled
* A question which leads us to Him who is Light through and for us who are nothing

~ Edmond Jabès

All the children come riding/ giddy up on lambs/ to see darling God

~ Else Lasker-Schuler

She uneasily gets out of her dress and underthings and she is a girl again . . .

~Ron Hansen

Teach me to care and not to care
Teach me to sit still
Hurry up please it's time

~T.S. Eliot

WANT

I want/ you to have/ this . . .

~Mirabai (trans. Daniel Ladinsky)

gopi: Mirabai's nickname for herself

pada: footprint, physical and metrical

What would you do with me
If I came 'in white'

but I can wait no more – wait
till my hazel hair is dappled –
~ Emily Dickinson, Master Letter 3

Hum-Sah: I am That

I want to see you more – Sir –
Wonder wastes my pound
You said I had no size to spare
~ Emily Dickinson, Master Letter 2

You will know the happiness of being inhabited by your God
~ Edmond Jabès

Light in it body
~ Ed Roberson

The soul is kissed by God in its innermost regions
~ Hildegard Von Bingen

CONCENTRATION, CON-PENETRATION
an instant/ of doubled pleasure, concentration/ con-/penetration
~ Cecilia Vicuña

from its coil
the base of
journeying upward
toward God
~ Elizabeth Gilbert

MUCH MADNESS (divinest Sense)

Much Madness is divinest Sense—
~ Emily Dickinson

As I write this, the noises in my head are so loud that I am beginning to wonder . . .
~ St. Teresa of Avila

Bhikkhu: monk
Dukkha: uneasy, disquieted

BURNING

What is to give light must endure burning.
~ Victor Frankl

In the hither world I lead you willingly along the light-bearing paths . . .
~ C. D. Wright

Himself himself diversify
~ Emily Dickinson

The Spirit tells you what to do
~ Dennis Covington, *Salvation on Sand Mountain*

Have you the little chest — to put the alive—in?
~ Emily Dickinson, Master Letter 3

Be shelled, eyes, with double dark
And find the uncreated light
~ G. M. Hopkins

Like a dry board
When it has been scorched
Lead us into his Blessed breast
Through his Sweet open side
~ Julian of Norwich

[But Christ loved] her more than [all the disciples] and used to kiss her [often]
~ Gospel of Philip

The lord our god is a
burning and consuming fire
~ Hebrews 12:29

There's a certain Slant of light/Winter Afternoons—
~ Emily Dickinson

Sweet disorder
I am a stupid creature
~ St. Teresa of Avila

UNDER LIGHT
Under the Light, yet under
~ Emily Dickinson

seeks the flaw in everything and loves the flaw
~ Jorie Graham

O to be self-balanced
Grand is the seen, the light, to me
~ Walt Whitman

After the ecstasy the laundry

~ Jack Kornfield

EXIT//afterglow

Exit/ at another point into the intense outer light.

~ Rena Rosenwasser, *Isle.* ©1992. Used with permission of Kelsey St. Press.

the rooster sings my awakening

I can't live in anything moving too fast

~ Eugène Guillevic (trans. Patricia Terry)

Adrinka symbol for hope:

"God, there is something in the heavens, let it reach my hands"

lifting belly is so strange

~ Gertrude Stein

(that cowde no letter)

~ Julian of Norwich

homlyhed

~ Julian of Norwich

When I saw that I and my body are not the same

~ Carla Harryman

unloose small bats and owls

~ Sylvia Plath

I am in you and

You are in me

~ Thich Nhat Hanh

HEATHER WOODS received an MFA in Poetry and Teaching from San Francisco State University and an MFA in Writing from the University of San Francisco. At Kenyon College, she received her BA in Comparative Poetics, where she served as Student Associate on the *Kenyon Review*, and founded *Persimmons* literary magazine. She presently serves as a reader for Kelsey Street Press in Berkeley. Her work is visible in *Jacket*, *How2*, and *Switchback*. Recently, she collaborated on a festchrift honoring Kathleen Fraser (Nightboat Books). In her non-tome-time, Heather teaches writing to students from kindergarten through college. A San Francisco Bay Area native and fifth generation Californian, Heather has dwelled in Ohio, Minnesota, and Grenoble. Right now, she lives with her husband and their pups on a relic farm along the California coastline. Here, in her writing room, she can hear the sounding Sea.

45962134R10071

Made in the USA
Charleston, SC
07 September 2015